Taylor,

Wishing you a life full of grace. I'm excited to work with you.

Blessings,
Decha D.

Presented to

....

From

....

Date

....

The gift of hospitality shown in the scriptures is brought to life in this book. Thank you for showing others the importance of this special gift of God.

- Pastor Denise Wilson, D.Min.

Dedra's God-given gift of hospitality is inspiring and evident in her work. I have worked with Dedra over the years and understand her love of bringing the light of Christ in her hospitality and community events. I am sure you will enjoy reading this book as she takes you through a real life journey through scripture and visual inspirations that will inspire all those that want to embrace the Spiritual Gift of Hospitality.

- Wendell Pierce, Actor

A Breath of Grace

Embracing the Spiritual Gift of Hospitality

By Dedra D. Faine

ERP Resources, Inc., Publishing and Media
McLean | New Orleans

Copyright © by Dedra Faine and Celebrations from the Soul a Division of ERP Resources, Inc., Publishing and Media

All rights reserved. No part of this book may be reproduced, stored in a retrieval system, or transmitted in any form or by any means—electronic, mechanical, photocopy, recording, scanning, or other—except for brief quotations in critical reviews or articles, without the prior written permission of the publisher.

For information about special discounts for bulk purchases, please contact ERP Resources, Inc. at (703) 776.9003.

ERP Resources, Inc.
8300 Greensboro Drive, Suite 800
McLean, Virginia 22102

Library of Congress Number: 2014914522

ISBN 0-9786382-1-2

Scripture taken from the Holy Bible, New International Version®. Copyright © 1973, 1978, 1984 by International Bible Society. Used by permission of Zondervan. All rights reserved.

Cover and Interior Design: Sara M. Yokie

Editor: Alanna Boutin

Photograph Credits:

Rodney Bailey | 10, 18, 21, 31, 50, 52, 53, 57, 61, 74, 77, 80, 83, 85, 111, 114, 117, 122, 125, 126, 132, 135,

Stephanie Huppert | Cover Image, Copyright Image, Dedication Image, Introduction Image, Back cover, 3, 7, 62, 64, 65, 73, 101, 121

Saskia Paulussen | 28, 33, 38, 39, 41, 43, 64, 65, 136, 137

Dedra Faine | 22, 23

Flower Design Provided by Edge Florals Event Designers | Cover Image, Copyright Image, Introduction Image, Backcover, 13, 28, 38, 41, 43, 55

Food Design Provided by A La Carte Catering + Event Design | 28, 33, 43

Printed in China
10 9 8 7 6 5 4 3 2 1

Dedication

To my loving parents, James and Mary Daniel,
my beautiful family, Roger, Govan, and Lauren Faine,
and my brother and creative muse, Forrest Daniel.
Thank you for your support and encouragement.
With love and gratitude, Dedra XO

Contents

INTRODUCTION
The Greatest Lesson of All
1

HEART ✧ A WORK IN PROGRESS
Transformation
11
This Little Light of Mine, I'm Going to Let It Shine . . .
19
The Golden Rule
29
Seasons
39

HOME ❧ SANCTUARY

The Welcoming Table
51

Friendship Retreat
63

Celebrations from the Soul Space
75

Martha, Martha, Martha ❧ Preparation & Fellowship
81

Part I – Planning for Your Guests
82

Part II – Recipes
96

Part III – Inspiring Hospitality Message
104

COMMUNITY ❧ WE ARE ALL CONNECTED

Light Your Candle
115

Heavenly Father ❧ Use Me
123

My Prayer for You
133

ACKNOWLEDGMENTS
138

Introduction

The Greatest Lesson of All

Trust in the Lord with all of your heart and lean not on your own understanding. In all ways acknowledge Him and He shall direct your path (Proverbs 3:5–6).

And since I, your Lord and Teacher, have washed your feet, you ought to wash each other's feet. I have given you an example to follow. Do as I have done to you (John 13:14–15).

When you open your heart to serve others, seek God first, and he will speak to you in various ways to lead you in the path to be faithful stewards here on this earth. What I have come to know is that when I seek God's direction and release my own human desire, it helps me gracefully walk and be obedient in God's divine plan for my life.

When I first started the journey of telling the story of the gift of hospitality, I started with my own preconceived ideas of what this message was all about. I wanted to tell the story of hospitality using my gifts and talents to glorify God in all my works. I began with the approach of wanting to showcase areas in what I knew how to do best, from setting a beautiful table, to creating the perfect invite, to being a welcoming host. However, my heart continued to tug at me, and people and situations presented themselves and I quickly realized that there was more to this story.

In order to have a better understanding of what hospitality was all about, I began to reflect, pray, and study the Word of God to understand the true depths of this beautiful form of discipleship. When my focus was straight on God, I was led by the Holy Spirit and my heart was open to receive all of the wonderful examples in His Word and examples of what He placed in my life. This is when it became very clear to me that hospitality is my ministry. God continues to lead, teach, and bless me each and every day as He lights my path as I seek to have a better understanding of Him. I soon discovered, as you will as well, that hospitality goes well beyond the aesthetics of having everything in place and prepared just so; it begins within your heart. The scripture, *Better a dry morsel, and quietness therewith, than a house full of sacrifices with strife (Proverbs 17:1)* tells us that if you are not at a place of peace and civility in your heart, then no matter what the hospitable act is, it will not be the light of Christ.

God gave me examples in the Bible such as Abraham, Lydia, Queen Esther, Martha and Mary, and a host of others. He provided earthly examples through my family, friends, and in my work. Through all of these examples, it became very clear to me that the journey of having a hospitable heart starts with the faith to have a heart of servitude to treat people the way you would want to be treated.

Acts of hospitality date back to the Old Testament, and then into the New Testament where travelers were openly received by hosts and hostesses called to open their homes in order to spread the message of faith. Without modern conveniences of hotels and restaurants, journeys were filled with random and miraculous tasks carried out by honorable and obedient heroines within households. The road of faith literally required everyone, from apostles, prophets, and missionaries, to rely upon the kindness of strangers placed along their paths to lighten their load, provide a loaf of bread, or just a warm bed for the night.

In the Old Testament, the father of many nations, Abraham, revealed his hospitable heart. *The Lord appeared to Abraham near the great trees of Mamre while he was sitting at the entrance to his tent in the heat of the day. Abraham looked up and saw three men standing nearby. When he saw them, he hurried from the entrance of his tent to meet them and bowed low to the ground. He said, "If I have found favor in your eyes, my lord, do not pass your servant by. Let a little water be brought, and then you may all wash your feet and rest under this tree. Let me get you something to eat, so you can be refreshed and then go on your way—now that you have come to your servant" (Genesis 18:2–5).* Abraham understood the blessing of having the company of these three men and faithfully provided hospitality during their stay. His faith was at the forefront of his hospitable discipleship and an example for generations to come.

In the New Testament, the soul of hospitality is Martha meets Lydia. Both of these women used hospitality to minister. Enchanting and powerful, their beguiling faith and glorious spirits of service to others inspire contemporary Christians today to unearth their gifts that reflect the light of Christ. By enhancing the beauty of our world, modern Marthas, Marys, Esthers, and a host of Lydias demonstrate that by loving their neighbors, friends, and family through a warm welcome, a simple meal of breaking bread, they provide hope by serving others the scriptural principle of graceful hospitable discipleship.

When I look back at my childhood, it is so clear how God used my grandmothers to provide a foundation for me in hospitable discipleship. Have you ever heard of the song, "Praying Grandmother"? I was blessed with two praying grandmothers that loved their families. They had a strong belief in the Word of God, and they displayed that in their daily lives. As a little girl growing up I knew this not just because they attended church weekly, sang in the choir, and served their churches in a variety of ways. I knew it because of their hospitable heart in how they put God first, and it was evident in the way they served others.

When I look back at both of them, I know their gracious spirits and unwavering faith was a clear reflection of the way they loved the Lord.

Any given Sunday, my grandma Marlow would have a house full of people from all walks of life that she was serving. She was an early riser and would wake up at 5:00 a.m. and cook dinner before she went to church. That way, if a minister, relative, neighbor, or stranger dropped by, she could serve a meal for them. Grandma's grace was in every heartbeat of the love that she shared with all those that she came in contact with. Her faithful obedience to serve others is the crowning glory of our family.

My grandma Daniel was a schoolteacher in the small town of Hillsboro, Virginia. She was known throughout the town as a woman who expected the best from each of her students. Just as she expected their best, she gave her best, not just in the classroom academically, but as a warrior for their well-being. When her students were hungry, needed clothing, shelter, school supplies, encouragement—you name it—she provided for them. She led by example, and her giving heart and spirit is a legacy that encourages me today as I walk in this journey to share the love of hospitality.

Throughout my adulthood, God has given me examples through my friends and associates at work. From working in the communities of New Orleans after Hurricane Katrina to serving in my community in Northern Virginia, I fully understand that during our darkest hours, we can make a difference by helping others.

When we receive our directions from God by showing love, compassion, and loyalty to our fellow man, we are God's beacon of light here on this earth. A faith-filled hospitable heart is achieved when one does not judge, is gracious, acknowledges, and loves others that come in their presence.

In this book, you will get the big picture. First, I will share God's Word through scripture which is so powerful in how He instructs us to be hospitable in our daily lives. Second, I will provide real-life examples of how God has used hospitable acts to make a difference in people's lives today. Third, in keeping with my gifts and talents in my love for making things look pretty and my love for hosting, I will provide beautiful visual inspirations and suggestions along the way to inspire your hospitable talents. Last, throughout each chapter, there will be an opportunity for you to participate in the building exercises toward your hospitable heart. The exercises will include three areas where you will *Pray, Practice, and Pen*.

I pray as you read this book, you will pause, receive, and reflect on the stories that are being told as examples for you. I pray that your heart will be transformed, that you will have a renewed spirit so that you will go out and be a beacon of light here on this earth, through acts of hospitable discipleship.

With love and gratitude,
Dedra Faine

SECTION I

Your Heart
A Work in Progress

Chapter 1
Transformation

Do not conform any longer to the pattern of this world, but be transformed by the renewing of your mind. Then you will be able to test and approve what God's will is—his good, pleasing and perfect will (Romans 12:2).

Therefore, as God's chosen people, holy and dearly loved, clothe yourselves with compassion, kindness, humility, gentleness and patience (Colossians 3:12).

I believe that God placed this book in your hand right at this moment in time because your heart is open and ready to be transformed to a higher place of awareness to be more hospitable in your life. When your heart is hospitable to God, His power and love become so evident in your life. My hope is for you to wake up in the morning, excited, knowing that He is using you and equipping you to do His wonderful works. This is such a wonderful feeling of empowerment given to us by the grace of our Almighty Father.

Search me, O God, and know my heart; test me and know my anxious thoughts. See if there is any offensive way in me, and lead me in the way everlasting (Psalm 139:23–24).

We live in a world where it feels like we are in a constant sense of attack. There are flashes of the dishevelment that go across our TV screens daily with the troubles of the world that we live in. This makes us feel disconnected with everyone, because unfortunately, the truth is, we are disconnected with ourselves. Over the years, I have found that when I settle down enough to start being quiet and go inward, that it is the perfect time for me to connect with myself, and it gives me an opportunity to assess my heart. Quite honestly, it is daily work for my thoughts and actions to be higher, for me to constantly want to be open to other people, for me to not judge my fellow man, and the list goes on.

The good news is when I get up in the morning and I am focused vertically on God and make that conscious decision to be clothed in His grace, my thoughts and actions are at a higher place of kindness, graciousness, nonjudgmental, loving and giving spirit. This is what my heart yearns for; however, let's face it . . . It is constant work, just like a marriage, a career, being a parent, a student, most importantly, a servant of God . . . In order to be good at it you have to work at it. The same applies with being a hospitable being. The first step is the renewing of your mind and spirit.

I remember years ago, I was in my early thirties when I was a stay-at-home mom. For some reason at that time, I started losing my voice, but in actuality, when I look back on it, my problem was that I couldn't hear God's voice. One night I had a dream that I was in a crowded room full of people and I was sitting in the back of the room and feeling out of place. All of a sudden, the Holy Spirit spoke to me and I stood up and said out loud to the crowd, "I've got the power within me." I instantly woke up from my dream and knew in my heart that God was speaking to me. *I can do everything through him who gives me strength (Philippians 4:13).* In that one instant my heart was transformed knowing that if I do the work, He will meet me wherever I am. Today, if you are ready to make that transformation to open your heart, be a beacon of God's light here on this earth, He is more than willing to walk with you. This is your time. Remember, if you practice it, it becomes who you are. You can do this ~ let's go!

Prayer

Dear Heavenly Father,

I awaken today to your presence and love, and I thank you. May your love guide me as I begin to transform my heart to be your servant on earth. Open my heart and my eyes to my surroundings. Let me not glide through this day, but let me be present and aware of you so my sight and your will, will be clearer to know the needs of others around me. Thank you for your unconditional love. Amen.

Practice

As you go about your week, take the time to observe others around you. Take mental notes to see if they are polite, judgmental, caring, uplifting, critical, unfriendly, loving, proactive to the needs of others, etc. You will be amazed at what you will find when you start paying attention.

Pen

What positive actions in others (i.e., family members, friends, community, strangers, etc.) as they interact with those around them did you see where you can grow from?

What negative actions did you see in yourself that was not of God's grace? The next time you have a negative action or feeling, how will you combat it?

What is your prayer for yourself as you begin this journey of being a hospitable disciple?

Chapter 2
This Little Light of Mine, I'm Going to Let It Shine …

You are the light of the world. A city on a hill cannot be hidden. Neither do people light a lamp and put it under a bowl. Instead they put it on its stand, and it gives light to everyone in the house. In the same way, let your light shine before men, that they may see your good deeds and praise your Father in heaven (Matthew 5:14–16).

You, O Lord, keep my lamp burning; my God turns my darkness into light (Psalm 18:28).

We are on a hospitable heart journey. Along the way, I want to give you tools to embrace and develop this calling on your life. What I know for sure is in order to give your best, you have to be at your best—mind, body, and spirit. One day I was dragging with little energy in my boot camp class at my local gym and Donna, my instructor, immediately asked me what I ate that morning. I told her I had some grapes on my car ride over. She told me that not eating enough that morning was like me traveling to downtown D.C. (about 45 minutes away) on an empty gas tank. That simple explanation resonated with me, moving over to our spiritual well-being. If we do not keep our pilot light lit with the light of Christ, we will go dim, and it's like driving on empty. Remember as I said earlier, in order to give our best, we have to be at our best.

The question is, how do you keep your tank on full? I understand that some days we teeter between full, half full, and sometimes empty. The critical part of this is understanding when your tank is not full and fueling it. I have incorporated different things in my life that fuels my spirit. *Your word is a lamp to my feet, and a light for my path (Psalms 119:105).*

There is a lake in my community where I go to enjoy the beautiful nature that surrounds it. Oftentimes I go there to pray, meditate, and to fuel my spirit. When I close my eyes I hear a peaceful symphony of birds and other animals amongst the evergreen trees, where the presence of God's omnificent power is so grand. In the mornings, I like to pray in a prostrate position (I lay facedown on my stomach and stretch my hands out). There is something about this position where I am humbled and am able to release my cares of the world to God, and I'm able to hear His voice.

Also, my Bible study group fuels my spirit. To be around a group of women wanting to grow and understand God's Word is rejuvenating every time I am in their presence. As I get older, I realize that to be at my best self I must exercise, eat right, and take care of my body. My friend Marcie runs six miles a day, and she uses that time of exercising as her prayer time with God.

Remember the mother in the airplane adage . . . When the masks drop in the airplane if you don't put the mask over your face first then you can't help your children. This concept applies here. You must keep your fire lit with the light of Christ in order to do his calling. It's a one-day-at-a-time process. It's about finding your own personal rhythm to keep your light shining brightly. This process is like setting your table. You do the work to create a beautiful setting, then you can come back to eat at that table and enjoy the beauty of it. Remember, if you do your work, your light will be lit, then you can go out and be a blessing to others.

Prayer

Dear Heavenly Father,

Thank you for your light and love, and the light in me. I pray for my mind to be focused and my soul to unite with your abundant light so that my path is bright and my way is clear. You are my salvation. Amen.

Practice

List four (4) things in your life that you may be already doing or need to incorporate in your life to brighten your light. Beside each item, write how you will make sure that these things are in your daily life.

1.

2.

3.

4.

Pen

After a few weeks of practicing your above items diligently, has this affected your light?

Moving forward, what will be your triggers to determine when your light is getting dim?

What can you consciously do to brighten it?

Chapter 3
The Golden Rule

Many are the plans in a man's heart, but it is the Lord's purpose that prevails (Proverbs 19:21).

He will reply, I tell you the truth, whatever you did not do for one of the least of these, you did not do for me (Matthew 25:45).

One of our greatest lessons when Jesus walked this earth was His humility and how He treated people and had concern for others. Remember the Golden Rule? Treat people the way you want to be treated. There are many ways that we can begin to let God's grace move. If we start off by opening our hearts and embracing that basic principle, "The Golden Rule," it will be the stepping-stone on our journey to make a difference through our actions as we become more hospitable in our lives.

One of my colleagues became ill, and I was offered the opportunity to begin to teach a civility course. As I began to teach the class, during my research and preparation, it became very clear to me of how hospitality and civility connect with each other. If we practice civility, we are being kind, attentive, aware, and the list goes on. Hospitality is an act of civility. Think about it, when we graciously open our homes and are active in uplifting our community, we are treating people the way we would want to be treated. When I realized this profound connection and the way this class came to me out of the blue, God's divine order and the story that He was preparing me for was crystal clear throughout this process.

I remember on the first day of class, I asked my students, "What does civility mean to you?" They answered, to treat people the way you want to be treated, be kind, show respect, caring for and serving others, acknowledge and listening, and the list continued. My heart was so excited to have the opportunity to teach a class that brought students' attention toward being hospitable stewards. *So in everything, do to others what you would have them do to you, for this sums up the Law and the Prophets (Matthew 7:12).* By serving others through hospitable acts we are obeying and honoring God.

In the world we live in, it's not easy to always be civil and hospitable beings. We live in trying times where we are overcompetitive, where we are rushed, where we are out of time and focused on ourselves. Unfortunately, we must all look in the mirror because that is our

truth. Let's face it, we are not perfect. With the best of intentions, things happen and we are not always the best we can be. However, what we know for sure is that God is perfect and that is why we should look to Him to guide us through this process.

How do we take the focus off of worldly things and problems? *It is the Lord your God you must follow, and him you must revere. Keep his commands and obey him; serve him and hold fast to him (Deuteronomy 13:4)*. We must not focus on the problems; we must focus on the solution . . . and that is our Heavenly Father.

So if we put all of our focus and follow God and let Him show us ways of how to seek His face in order to be more accepting and gracious toward our fellow man, will that actually work? What I have found to be true is that when we take that step of faith toward God, He takes leaps and bounds toward us.

I gave an assignment for my students to be more accepting and gracious toward others. I asked them to be open and receptive to their surroundings by showing grace and kindness throughout their week at home and to strangers. I gave this assignment, and I anxiously waited for their responses, but the first person to speak was me. I couldn't help myself. My week was blessed tenfold because I actively engaged in the assignment myself. That whole week I was on alert about how I could serve someone through my actions. It was a blessing to know when I have a grace-filled heart, God will allow me to be used in many different ways.

During that week, I didn't have to donate thousands of dollars. All I had to do was smile graciously, listen attentively, say hello to strangers, slow down in the car and allow people in front of me. I just needed to be patient while waiting in lines, hold the door for a group of students, help a new mom to her car with groceries, deliver flowers to my sick neighbor, etc. I believe that by doing these simple acts of kindness, God was sharpening my hospitable skills, thus, giving me the heart of a servant. The more that I dwelled in civility, the grace of hospitality became clearer.

People often equate civility with good manners. One interesting rule for good etiquette at a table is that the salt and pepper shaker always travel together on the table. If someone asks for the pepper, you pass the salt as well. Basically, in a hospitable way, you are showing empathy toward others by being aware of their needs just in case they decide that they need the salt in addition to the pepper. *Therefore, as God's chosen people, holy and dearly loved, clothe yourselves with compassion, kindness, humility, gentleness and patience (Colossians 3:12).* The salt and pepper shaker, although a simple example, have profound meanings. When we honor and serve and have empathy toward our fellow man, we honor and serve God in the process.

You can be the beacon of light by showing grace, love, and empathy to your fellow man. Today, start focusing on being civil and compassionate by doing the simple things to make a difference. It starts changing your heart. Trust me, the end result will be a huge blessing in your life as you embrace the principles of hospitable discipleship. *And over all these virtues put on love, which binds them all together in perfect unity (Colossians 3:14).*

Prayer

Dear Heavenly Father,

Lead my heart to be more civil toward others. Give me the courage to reach out and help my fellow man. Give me the insight to know of others' needs before they know it themselves. Teach me to be a better steward of your light and love through the grace of hospitable discipleship. Amen.

Practice

Meditate and pray on the Word. "Let love guide your life" (Colossians 3:14) and consciously take your blinders off (i.e., turn off your earphones or your phone when going into a store, be observant of your neighbors, find time to sit together at the dinner table with your family and friends, etc.). During this time, be aware of how God provides for your own needs and, in turn, focus on how you can serve others and be a light here on this earth.

Pen

List examples of how God provides for your needs.

What did you do to serve the needs of others, and how did they react?

How do the actions of being aware of other people raise your awareness toward having a hospitable heart?

Chapter 4
Seasons

There is a time for everything, and a season for every activity under heaven (Ecclesiastes 3:1).

We all go through different seasons in our life that may encompass harvest, hibernation, blossom, or renewal. Whatever season that you are going through, from the most joyful times to times of suffering, there is always time to make a difference in someone's life through God's grace.

Many times in our lives we make excuses of why we are unable to be hospitable toward others. Maybe it's financial, or we feel our home is not in order, or we are too busy; the list is endless. The reality—God can use you no matter where you are in your life. You don't have to be Cathy Chatty to smile and say hello to someone, or have the financial resources to throw a lavish spread, or have your tank full. God meets you where you are. If your heart is open to receive what God wants you to do, no matter what your circumstance, if He sends it to you, He will see you through it. Being present and in the moment allows us to capture the blessing of God's will in our life.

Have you ever been in a situation where you get the whisper or a tug at your heart, and you know in that instant that you need to do something. *One of those listening was a woman named Lydia, a dealer in purple cloth from the city of Thyatira, who was a worshiper of God. The Lord opened her heart to respond to Paul's message. When she and the members of her household were baptized, she invited us to her home. If you consider me a believer in the Lord," she said, "come and stay at my house." And she persuaded us. She was a worshiper of God. The Lord opened her heart to respond to Paul's message (Acts 16:14–15).* I love the story of Lydia because she reminds me of a modern-day woman. She owned her own business, she ran her household, and I'm quite sure in doing all of that she was quite a busy lady. However, as the story goes, she worshiped God, and the Lord opened her heart to pay attention and listen to what Paul was saying. After hearing Paul speak, she decided to have her whole household baptized. She then preceded to welcome Paul and his companions to come into her home. *Come and stay in my house if you have*

decided that I am a true believer in the Lord" (Acts 16:15). She shows the power of an open heart to be used to serve at God's will.

My mentor, Linda Higgison, once said to me that no matter where you are in life, whether good or bad, you know you have reached a place of peace when you know it's a blessing from God. That speaks to my soul so much, because at the end of the day, whether I'm on the mountaintop or in the valley, God has work for me to do. I just have to put him first and walk with an open heart to hear His voice.

My brother Forrest was in the hospital and at that time was recovering from what was a near-death experience. In that moment of recovery, with tubes running in and out of his body, God still spoke to his heart and told him although he was in that place, he could still be a blessing and shine God's beautiful light. He said he began to pray for the nurses and the technicians that were servicing him. What I found in the hospital is that these nurses and technicians have a calling themselves. What they do to serve their patients is a gift from God. They work extremely hard and a lot of times we saw that they were overwhelmed. He said that the nurses told him that he made their day and they needed his prayers. During his stay in the hospital, his prayers lifted many people that came in his path. That shows us that in any situation we can be used, and in the darkest hours of your life, there is still light for you to give to others.

No matter where you are . . . if you are lying in a hospital bed like Forrest, standing on the street like Lydia, wherever, God will call upon you to serve. I challenge you today through the power of the Holy Spirit to commit to do your part in restoring the faithful and loving discipleship of hospitality to our world.

Prayer

Dear Heavenly Father,

I pray for my heart to be open to be used for the perfect task that you have for me at this very moment. Let my heart be filled with your light, let my actions be of your love, let all that I am be of you. Amen.

Practice

As you go about your day, know in your heart that God will use you in many ways. Take time to listen to a friend, pray with a neighbor, hold the door for a stranger, the key is to be open and consciously make an effort to be a blessing to others. Remember it doesn't cost a penny to be kind and gracious to all that come in our path.

Pen

Living with a hospitable heart, how has it affected your being?

Where are you in your spiritual life of being hospitable and open to others?

List ways where you have started to be more hospitable and open to others and the affects that it has on your life?

SECTION II

Home ☙ Sanctuary

Chapter 5
The Welcoming Table

A loving atmosphere in your home is the foundation for your life (Chinese Proverb).

Creating a welcoming sanctuary where God's light and love is at the center is a wonderful recipe for a hospitable home. We live in a world filled with busy schedules and activities that often leave us overwhelmed. That is why it is so crucial that we create an environment within our home where the dwellers can come and get their refuge. It is also crucial for us to pray for the heart of the dwellers. If we are soiled on the inside before we go out into the world, we will not have the proper foundation to sustain us.

It is important to create a strong foundation of Christ within your home. Developing practices and rituals for your family that honor and bring the light of Christ, helps to build a home that thrives on love. When I was growing up, my parents strongly believed that children should have routines. They established routines for us even when we were young adults, where we came together and sat at the table for dinner every night and breakfast on weekends. My parents thought it was very important for us to commune, pray, eat, and share our thoughts and daily activities. I think one of the biggest impacts for me was the act of bringing us all to the table. It allowed us to lay a foundation in our lives that encouraged prayer and family time. This is something that my family cherished over the years, and it has now extended into our next generation. By bringing us to the table together, we learned how to pray and give thanksgiving to God, we learned good table manners, and we shared family history and skills that we can take out into the world. *Your wife shall be like a fruitful vine within your house, your children like olive plants around your table (Psalm 128:3).* The simple acts and lessons at the table are phenomenal blessings that we can extend to our family, roommates, and our guests.

If we keep God in our hearts first, then everything we do in our home can be of his loving spirit. When you do tasks for your love of Christ, in preparation for your family to have time together around your table, the routine activities suddenly are filled with the light of Christ. When you are cooking dinner for your family, setting the table and/or cleaning up afterward, do it as unto the Lord and for His glory, then all of the burdens of your tasks will be lifted. In turn, your family will be blessed because you are preparing with a grateful and love-filled heart knowing that it is for the glorification of Jesus. This love of Jesus extends into your family and household. This spirit of love, grace, and worship of God will extend when each person walks out of our home.

When I was on tour with my first book, *Celebrations from the Soul: an Inspirational Sourcebook for Personal Entertaining,* a mom with busy teenagers came up to me and said that she was blessed by the hospitality message; however, she and her family have such a busy schedule that they are like ships passing each other during the night. Yet, her heart was yearning for that time for her family to commune together and share their time around the table. After brainstorming and coming up with different solutions, we came up with dessert time. During dessert time, perhaps it's 8:00 p.m., they would light a candle for the light of Christ, pray, and discuss what was going on in each of their lives. She walked away with hope, understanding that there is no cookie-cutter way of going about this. The key is finding the best solution for your family. Even if you have roommates, or you are single, it is up to you to figure out ways that your house is centered with the light of Christ so that all who come to your table will walk away blessed. Remember, this is the foundation that will spread to the world when they walk outside of your doors.

Prayer

Dear Heavenly Father,

I pray that the Holy Spirit dwells in my home. Let all of us sit at your table of grace with love, worship, and humility. Amen.

Practice

Sweets & Treats (Fellowship Time)

Create a table where people will come and feel special. Can you imagine, it's 8 p.m., and everyone is home, homework is done, bath time is behind you, and everyone has their pajamas on. You call your family downstairs, and they see a special table for them made by you filled with special treats. They all gather around with great excitement and as parents, you share with them how special they are to you. Then you proceed to light candles that are on the table to let them know the candle signifies the light of Christ. You then proceed to pray together and share and fellowship with the family that God has bestowed upon you over special treats. (i.e., a hot chocolate bar with special treats would be fun, or if you want to do snacks that do not include sugar, that is an option as well). I don't know about you, but this gets me a lot of brownie points with my family, and at the end of the day, we are all blessed by it. Whether you have children, or you may be single, this can be a special time of sharing and fellowship with the ones that you love. Remember, hospitality begins at home.

Pen

What can you discuss at the table to share the love of God in your family's life?

Ask your family for their input on creative rituals/practices that they would like to see and share at the table and within other areas of your home.

Find scriptures that you would like to share around your table. You will be blessed.

Chapter 6
Friendship Retreat

Create in me a clean heart, O God, and renew a steadfast spirit within me (Psalm 51:10).

Take my yoke upon you and learn from me, for I am gentle and humble in heart, and you will find rest for your souls (Matthew 11:29).

Extending hospitality to your sisters in Christ is always a wonderful opportunity to serve and glorify God in our daily lives. As women we play many roles in our lives, from being daughters and servants of Christ, moms, wives, sisters, friends, daughters, employees, business owners, teachers, coaches, volunteers, therapists, prayer warriors, and the list goes on. Sometimes all of these roles can get us off centered. It is important that we step out of the race to get rejuvenated. Creating a retreat in the company of our friends is the perfect setting in order for us to be refueled to run the race that God has set before us. *Therefore, since we are surrounded by such a great cloud of witnesses, let us throw off everything that hinders and the sin that so easily entangles, and let us run with perseverance the race marked out for us (Hebrews 12:1).*

My refuge when I am weary is often spent with my girlfriends. We pray together, laugh, pray again, and get through tough times together. Have you ever shared a special time with your dear friends who are kindred spirits, where the busy world that encompasses your daily life . . . stops for a moment? A time and space that is harmonious in nature and the

energy source that flows is of God's grace. A time where the comfort of your surroundings with cherished friends gives you the opportunity to rest your spirit and seek comfort in each other and a higher power in order to restore your physical, mental, emotional, and spiritual well-being.

Over the years I have been fortunate to share special times with my dearest of friends, where we have gathered together with the expectation to relax and enjoy one another's company, and the outcomes are always gratifying and uplifting, to say the least. Those spaces and places where we stepped into serenity are places where many words are not spoken, but a lot is said through our fervent prayers. I believe these special times spent with friends are confirmations of God's intention to provide angels on earth to help nurture our spirits as we walk in the bond of sisterhood. These special moments help us to rejuvenate ourselves so we can be at our best as we walk in our journey to fulfill all of the roles that God has given us.

Prayer

Heavenly Father,

I pray that my home can be a place where my sisters in Christ can come and find rest. I pray that my heart is open and receptive to those that are in need. As I plan my friendship retreat, let me seek you in my planning so I can glorify you. I pray to focus vertically on you to understand your will and guide me to serve your dear daughters. Amen.

Practice

It would be a blessing to create a retreat for your friends to prepare them for heightened seasons of their lives. I have provided an example of how to create a retreat within your home.

First, during a friendship retreat, it is important to touch all of the five senses: hear, touch, smell, sight, and taste. You should send an invitation to your friends. In the invitation you want to outline not only the basic details of date, time, and place, but you want to tell the story of what the retreat will entail.

The invitation needs to be visual in a sense that it shows calmness through colors, wording, etc. For this occasion, you can get an invitation that shows peace through scripture, a poem, a water stream, a sunset, or relaxing colors like olive or light blue. In addition, come up with a creative caption, such as "Leave the Cares of the World Behind" to help engage your guests so that the excitement of having the opportunity to relax and spend time with friends starts as soon as they receive the invitation. With my friends we have so many obligations, that it takes a special invitation to get them moving so that everything can be in place so they literally can leave the cares of the world behind them.

Second, focus on creating the right ambiance in your home. You want to welcome your guests by creating a spalike atmosphere as soon as they arrive. Dim your lights and display on a table beautiful candles that will illuminate their pathway into your home. Adding a water fountain in that area will add another sensory effect. Also, display a unique container filled with comfortable slippers that your guests can put on as they start their journey to relaxation. In addition, appeal to their sense of hearing by softly playing a CD where you can enjoy music that is comforting for the soul.

Third, center the retreat in an area of your home that is most comfortable for lounging. Typically, that would be your great room. In that room, display low arrangements (so you can have full eye contact with everyone in the room). Some suggestions to enhance the ambience are bamboo plants, orchids, rocks, etc. Of course, candles, candles, candles should be the main light source of your room. This will create a nice glow throughout the space. In addition, have a wicker basket full of plush blankets that your guests can cuddle up to. Other than that, keep it very simple because you do not want to overstimulate your guests with too much activity in décor. You want to keep it calm and simple.

Fourth, plan a simple menu that is refreshing and light that can be prepared ahead of time with little work the day of your retreat. Oftentimes, we are bombarded with heavy caloric foods. Make this day light with special treats that promote your physical well-being. Remember, this retreat is to nurture your soul as well, so consider hiring a caterer and a server to help on that day. This will ensure that your guests will have time to enjoy your company and you will have time to enjoy theirs and relax.

Fifth, bring in a speaker that encourages your spiritual nourishment, a masseuse, a manicurist, and an esthetician. This will leave your guests feeling alive, pretty, and leaping back into the world with renewed energy to finish God's race with love and light.

Pen

1. Who will you invite to your retreat?

2. Out of your circle of friends, what would they want as special treats (i.e., masseuse, guest speaker, food, etc.)?

3. Write down scriptures, a special message, or poem that would be the foundation of your special retreat and its purpose. How can you relay this message throughout your retreat?

4. What is your idea of an ultimate friends retreat? Answer these questions: Who, What, When, Where, Why.

Chapter 7
Celebrations from the Soul Space

Trust in the Lord with all your heart and lean not on your own understanding; in all your ways acknowledge him, and he will make your paths straight (Proverbs 3:5–6).

As we go throughout our year, we will come to seasons where we will be busier than others. From the start of the school year, Thanksgiving, Christmas, all the way into the New Year, our gears are on high. Over the years, as I walked through my busy seasons that encompassed the hustle and bustle of life, I found myself not at peace. I was in the spirit of keeping up with schedules to plan parties, decorate the house, coordinate school functions, etc. It was often overwhelming, especially as a young mother.

Over time I realized that I am my best self when I am centered and at a pace that is soothing to my spirit. Trying to do it all when you lose yourself in the schedule of the tasks at hand is a disservice to your soul. It brings on extra anxiety that trickles out to the ones you love most, and it is not what God wants us to do. *And the peace of God, which transcends all understanding, will guard your hearts and your minds in Christ Jesus (Philippians 4:7).* What I have found is when I stay focused on God and let Him be my guide each and every day to determine what should be done, and when it should be done, then I'm on the right course for internal peace.

Taking the time to stop and quiet yourself to listen to God with an open heart is truly a blessing. It brings joy, peace, and ultimately, God's will into your being. A special gift that you can give to yourself is to create what I call the "Celebrations from the Soul Space." This is your space within your home to have your quiet moments with yourself and God, to pray, meditate, or whatever your heart desires. This space will be your reminder to take your rest with God each and every day.

Prayer

Dear Heavenly Father,

I pray that I remind myself of the importance of my one-on-one time with you. I pray that my spirit will quiet itself to understand your will in my life. Amen.

Practice

Personal "Celebrations from the Soul Space"

Imagine a space that when you enter, you instantly take a deep breath and release all that does not move you in a positive space. This beautiful soul space is your way of honoring God and yourself. It will give you the opportunity to have some alone time with your Creator. This time is essential to your well-being, especially when we are embarking on a busy season. Have a space, whether it is indoors or outdoors, that feels good to your spirit. There are no rights and wrongs, because what pampers your soul is an individual blessing.

Pen

Where will you create your "Celebrations from the Soul Space"?

....

....

....

....

What time will you make each day to go to your space?

....

....

....

....

What specialty items will you bring to this space that will infuse the light of God into your space?

....

....

....

....

Chapter 8
Martha, Martha, Martha ❧ Preparation & Fellowship

As Jesus and his disciples were on their way, he came to a village where a woman named Martha opened her home to him. She had a sister called Mary, who sat at the Lord's feet and listened to what he said. But Martha was distracted with all the preparations that had to be made. She came to him and asked, "Lord, don't you care that my sister has left me to do the work by myself? Tell her to help me!" "Martha, Martha," the Lord answered, "you are worried and upset about many things, but only one thing is needed. Mary has chosen what is better, and it will not be taken from her"
(Luke 10:38–42).

Part I
Planning for Your Guests

Do nothing out of selfish ambition or vain conceit, but in humility consider others better than yourselves (Philippians 2:3). We hear the Martha and Mary story over and over and how Martha was so busy in preparation that she neglected to focus on Jesus who was her guest. Often our modern-day Marthas get flack on their so-called perfectionist style of entertaining. Is it prideful entertaining or is it just that everyone has their own way in how they want to serve their guests? Who are we to judge? At the end of the day, Jesus said to be attentive to your guests, so that should be number one. Also, it is important for us to create an atmosphere where our guests feel welcome in our home, so the key is to create a balance between Martha and Mary. One great way to help with this is to have solid preparation so when your guests enter, you are open to fellowship with them.

As you begin preparation, let the love of God guide you. All that follows will be gravy . . . if we keep our hearts in the right place.

Prayer

Dear Heavenly Father,

I pray for clarity over the intention of my hospitality. Let me be mindful of my guests and use this as an opportunity to serve you, so that I may serve them. Amen.

Practice

Here are some suggestions on how to prepare so you can be attentive to your guests:

- Begin with prayer and ask God to lead you in your preparation.
- When you start to plan, create a timeline with dates and action items so you aren't running around at the last minute. This gives you a guide to prepare with little stress. When creating my plan for hosting, these are the items that I consider (i.e., guest list, invitations, food, entertainment, flowers, table scapes, and rentals). If I have a lot of people, I will go to my local rental company to get silverware, china, linen, etc. Here is the layout of my timeline:

Date/Task/Person Responsible/Notes

- If you are new to hosting people in your home, keep your guest numbers at an adequate level so that you do not feel overwhelmed. Remember, the more you practice hosting, it will become easier.

❧ Create an invitation that engages your guests and gives them a feel of what will be. Here are important things to remember for your invitation:

- Proofread: Title, location, date, time, RSVP date, guests' names.
- If you are unsure of how to format your invitation, visit specialty stationary stores in person or online—there are tons of ideas out there that you can tap into.
- Remember to indicate if it is a surprise.
- Choose an unusual invitation size that does not look like your guests' other mail.
- At the post office, check the weight and make sure to apply enough postage.
- The post office also has a variety of stamps—pick one that complements your event.
- Consider using a calligrapher—it truly will be a unique touch for your party.
- Have someone else proofread the invitation for you. Another trick is to read the invitation backward. You can catch typos that way.
- If not obvious, let guests know what attire is required.
- Include parking details if you have valet, etc.

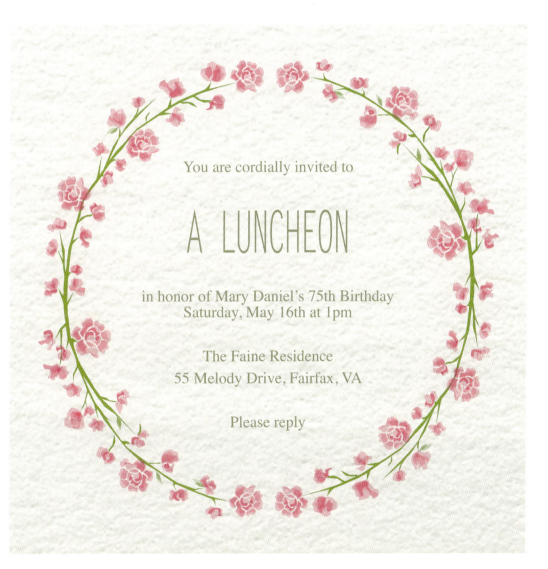

- Open your invitation list to others outside of people that you may know. Maybe there is a widowed man/woman or new neighbor that you can invite over. Keep your heart open and listen to God and He will let you know who needs to be on your invite list.
- Create a menu that requires little preparation on the day of the event or hire a caterer and/or waiter to help in the service. I have found over the years that when my budget allows, my caterer takes off all of the pressure of being in two places at one time. On these occasions, I can put my Mary hat on and be fully engaged in the celebration with my guests.
- Prepare your table.
    - How to set a table *(see diagram on page 91)*
    - Flowers (a good sustainable practice is to research local flower growers in your area).
    - Linens (a beautiful table linen is like wearing that perfect dress and adds a lot of character to your table).
    - Specialty items that make your table unique (i.e., during special occasions I like to add items to the table that add character or tell a story, through scripture, seasonal pieces, pictures, etc.).

- If you need seating for a multitude of people, set up different tables in your home in different shapes (i.e., round, square, oval, rectangular) that can be decorated differently, yet, tell the same story with complimenting tablescapes.

❧ Have a plan on how you want your gathering to flow.

❧ Get dressed two hours prior to your guests' arrival. It allows for any last-minute problems that may arise.

❧ No space is too small. The best celebrations are the most intimate ones.

❧ Last but not least, remember, true hospitality should be reflective of God's Spirit. Keep this thought at the forefront and you will be on your way to create Celebrations from the Soul.

When I was growing up my main chore for my family was that I had to set the table every night for dinner. It's funny how God prepares you; what looked like a chore as a child was my preparation for my destiny to share the Spiritual Gift of Hospitality. These are some table setting tips that I have picked up along the way. I created this table setting/scape outline based on the average number of courses (three to four) that I serve in my home when I am hosting. In the illustration that I am providing the courses would include: (1) Soup course, (2) Salad, (3) Entrée and (4) Dessert.

- The rule of thumb is that utensils are placed in the order of use from the outside in.
- The majority of the time with a few exceptions, forks go to the left of the plate and knives and spoons go to the right.
- Your dinner plate is the anchor of your setting. I always anchor the dinner plate by placing it one inch from the edge of the table.
- Place the two forks to the left of the plate. In this case, the smaller fork for the salad would be on the outside of the larger dinner fork, because that is the order in which you will be eating. Salad first. Remember, utensils are placed in the order of use from the outside in.
- The napkin is placed either on the left side of the plate folded or on top of the plate. This is one piece that varies based on how the host wants to decorate their table. I have seen where people will put

Celebrations from the Soul

the napkin under the plate or in a glass. This is where your creative juices can flow in deciding the best place as far as aesthetics are concerned.

- The dinner knife is set immediately to the right of the plate. Always remember that the sharp edge goes toward the plate. If the main course is meat, a steak knife can take place of the dinner knife.
- Spoons go to the right of the dinner knife. The illustration shows where the soup is, which is served first. Also, please note that the dessert or teaspoon is inside of the soup spoon because that serving will be after the soup course.
- Glasses (water, wine, juice, iced tea) – are placed at the top right of the dinner plate, directly above the knives and spoons. The water goblet is the first glass above the knife.
- Salad plate is placed to left of the forks.
- Bread plate with butter knife goes directly above the forks with the butter knife place diagonally across the plate.
- The dessert fork and spoon can be placed at the top of the plate horizontally (the spoon on the top with its handle facing to the right; the fork below with its handle facing left); or beside the plate. If you choose to place the dessert fork and spoon beside the plate, the fork would go to the left closest to the plate because it will be used last. The spoon would go to the right side of the plate, to the right of the dinner knife and to the left of the soup spoon.

- Coffee cups and saucers are oftentimes brought out with dessert and would be placed to the right of the knives and spoons. If you choose to pre-set the cup and saucer then you would place it to the right of the knife and spoons.
- Extra details that make your table special:
- Place cards can be a great accent to your table and enhance your décor while keeping everyone organized.
- Candles are a great way to create ambiance and light within your room.
- Flowers are perfect for a beautiful tablescape. Always remember to keep the arrangements at a level where guests can see one another.
- Fresh fruit, leaves, pictures, etc., all enhance the beauty of your table. I look at a table like a pretty little black dress where it is all about how you accessorize it. You can dress it up or keep it simple. The options are limitless to tell your story when hosting.

Pen

Pray for the vision of an opportunity where you can be a blessing to others while hosting them in your home. Answer these questions: Who, What, When, Where, and Why. Use the planning tips above to help you in the implementation of your vision.

....

....

....

....

....

....

....

....

....

....

....

....

....

Part II

Recipes

Throughout this book we have described several instances in the Old Testament, New Testament, and in our modern times where sharing a meal with others was an essential part of being hospitable. When people come into your home, whether they are expected or they just show up, it always enriches the fellowship when you can share something from your kitchen. I often think of my aunt Mary Basil (we affectionately call her Aunt Mutt) at 94 years of age. No matter when you come to visit she will always offer you something to eat. One year during the Christmas holiday, my mom and I visited Aunt Mutt with the expectations to come and fellowship and enjoy her company. The next thing we knew, Aunt Mutt pulled out all of this food from the Christmas holiday and set the most beautiful table for us. As we gathered around her table, eating and sharing stories, we felt so special to sit in her company as her niece and grandniece, fully understanding the blessing of that moment. Aunt Mutt is old school, and it is remarkable how she gets around. Her legacy is a part of the grand foundation that was set for our family to understand the graceful discipleship of hospitality.

My sister Corlessia (aka Cori) is such a wonderful cook and host. Whenever we come to visit her, often unexpected, she can always go and whip up something quickly for us where we are extremely happy with the results. She has shared some of her recipes that I think will help you as you prepare for your guests. These recipes are good staples because you can freeze them or cook them quickly, so no matter who shows up, you can break bread with them. Enjoy!

SALMON STEAKS WITH MANGO SALAD
All I can say is this is absolutely delicious. I love my sister's cooking!

Ingredients - Mango Salad

1 15-ounce can black beans
2 large mangos or papayas (diced)
1 small red onion
　(chopped to yield ¼ cup)
1 whole red or yellow bell pepper
1 jalapeño (diced)
1 medium garlic clove (minced)
3 tablespoons white vinegar
1 teaspoon sugar
Juice of ½ lime
⅛ teaspoon salt
Fresh pepper to taste

Directions

Combine all ingredients. Chill 1 hour before serving over salmon steaks

Ingredients - Salmon Steaks

Four salmon steaks, 1½-inch thick
2 cups onion, minced
4 tablespoons butter
¼ cup parsley, minced
2 tablespoons lemon juice
½ teaspoon salt
⅛ teaspoon pepper

Directions

Sauté onion in butter in a skillet over medium heat for 5 minutes until golden brown and limp. Mix in parsley and lemon juice. Sprinkle steaks with salt and pepper. Place in a shallow roasting pan. Spread the onion mixture on top of each steak. Cover the pan snugly with foil. Bake at 350 degrees for 10 minutes. Then uncover and bake 15 to 20 minutes or until the fish flakes. These may be grilled. Top with salsa over cooked salmon steaks. YUMMY!

LAVENDER ICE CREAM

Corlessia created this lavender ice cream because of my grandmother Marlow's love of lavender.

Ingredients

3 cups milk
3 stems of fresh lavender flowers
8 extra-large egg yolks
1½ cups white sugar
3 cups heavy cream

Directions

Heat the milk and lavender in a medium saucepan over low heat until warmed through. Remove from the heat, and allow lavender to infuse for about 25 minutes. Remove flowers (optional). I like the specs of flowers!

Beat the egg yolks and sugar together in a large bowl. Whisk the lavender-infused milk into the egg mixture, then pour it back into the saucepan.

Heat the mixture over low heat 7 to 10 minutes, whisking constantly until the mixture thickens and can coat the back of a spoon. Remove from the heat and cool slightly, about 5 minutes. Then stir in the heavy cream.

Transfer the mixture to a bowl and chill in the refrigerator at least 4 hours. Then pour the chilled mixture into an ice-cream maker and freeze according to the manufacturer's directions until it reaches "soft-serve" consistency.

Transfer the ice cream to a lidded container; cover the surface with plastic wrap and seal. For best results, ice cream should be placed in the freezer at least 2 hours or overnight. It can be frozen up to 2 months.

A CHOCOLATE GOOEY DELISH TREAT

Enjoy a taste of chocolate. This is the perfect treat for your girlfriends. Who doesn't love chocolate? Enjoy!

Ingredients

1 stick plus 1 tablespoon unsalted butter
4 ounces semisweet chocolate
2 extra-large eggs, room temperature
¾ cup superfine sugar
3 tablespoons all-purpose flour
4 (1-cup capacity) ramekins

Directions

Place a baking sheet in the oven and preheat to 400 degrees F. Butter the ramekins with 1 tablespoon of butter.

Either in a microwave or in a double boiler, melt the dark chocolate and 1 stick of butter, then set aside to cool slightly.

In another bowl, mix the eggs with the sugar and flour with a hand whisk and beat in the cooled butter and chocolate mixture. Divide the mixture between the 4 buttered ramekins. Bake for about 20 minutes. The tops will be cooked and cracked and the chocolate gooey underneath.

Place each ramekin on a small plate with a teaspoon and serve. Make sure to warn people that these desserts will be very hot and very gooey and very good... delish!!!

LEMON CAKE

This is a great cake that is wonderful to cook and freeze and pull out at a moment's notice to serve a special treat to your guests.

Ingredients

- 2 sticks plus 1 tablespoon room temperature unsalted butter
- 2½ cups sugar divided
- 4 eggs plus 1 egg yolk, room temperature, extra-large eggs
- ¼ cup lemon zest
- 3 cups flour
- ½ teaspoon baking powder
- ½ teaspoon baking soda
- 1 teaspoon salt
- ¾ cup lemon juice (preferably fresh)
- ¾ cups Half and Half or buttermilk, room temperature
- 1 teaspoon vanilla extract

Moisture for Cake
(Lemon Simple syrup)

- ½ cup granulated sugar
- ½ cup lemon juice

Add sugar and lemon juice in a small saucepan; heat on medium temperature until fully combined and all sugar is dissolved.

Glaze

- 2½ cups confectionary sugar
- 4 tablespoons lemon juice

Directions

Preheat oven to 350 F.
Grease and flour 2 loaf pans. In a large bowl, cream butter and 2 cups of sugar 5 minutes until light and fluffy. Add eggs one at a time. Then add lemon juice.

In a medium bowl, sift flour, baking powder, baking soda, and salt.

In a small bowl, add ¼ cup lemon juice, Half and Half or buttermilk, and 1 teaspoon of vanilla. Add the wet ingredients to the dry ingredients, alternatively, and mix. Pour the final mixture into the two loaf pans. Bake 40–45 minutes.

Remove the cakes from the oven. Let rest for 5 minutes, then remove the cakes from the loaf pans. Spoon Lemon Simple syrup over the cakes and let them soak for approximately 10 minutes. Place the cakes on wire racks to finish cooling. After cool, add lemon glaze to the cakes.

Glaze directions

Combine lemon juice and confectionary sugar. Pour over the cakes and let the glaze trickle over the sides. To you from me!!!! ENJOY!

To freeze for later use
Place lemon iced cake in the freezer until the icing hardens. Then wrap in plastic wrap or greaseproof paper and finish with a layer of aluminum foil. Can last in the freezer up to 2 months.

SUPER BOWL GUMBO

I lived in New Orleans and came back and told my sister that she has to make gumbo. I have tasted many versions of gumbo by living in the Crescent City, and this is one of my favorites. Bon appétit!

Ingredients

¼ cup oil
6 tablespoons all-purpose flour
2 cups onion, chopped
1 cup green bell pepper, chopped
1 cup celery, diced
3 large garlic cloves, minced
4 cups chicken broth
1 tablespoon chicken base
3 cups water
2 bay leaves
1½ teaspoons dried thyme
1 teaspoon dried basil
1/3 cup dried parsley
1 teaspoon lemon pepper
½ teaspoon cayenne pepper
2 teaspoons House Seasoning
2 tablespoons Worcestershire sauce
1 (14½-ounce) can diced tomatoes seasoned with garlic, basil, and oregano or 2 cups fresh diced tomatoes
4 cups sliced smoked turkey sausages Cajun
4 cups cut okra (fresh) (fried in vegetable oil and dried on paper towels)
2 pounds lump crabmeat
1½ pounds fresh peeled shrimp
3 cups bay scallops
Filé powder

Directions

In a large pot combine oil and flour. Cook over medium heat, stirring constantly until the roux has browned to a light caramel color. Add onion, pepper, celery, and garlic. Sauté for 2 to 3 minutes, stirring constantly. Slowly add chicken broth and chicken base, stirring constantly. Add water, bay leaves, thyme, basil, parsley, lemon pepper, cayenne pepper, House Seasoning, soy sauce, and tomatoes. Cut sausage into ½-inch pieces. Add to the pot along with fried okra. Cover the pot and simmer for 1 to 1½ hours, stirring occasionally. Add crabmeat, shrimp, and scallops. Simmer for an additional 15 minutes. Serve over jasmine rice. Sprinkle with filé powder on top of the bowl and stir in. Optional: garnish with blue crab claws.

House Seasoning:
1 cup salt, ¼ cup black pepper, ¼ cup garlic powder

Tip: Add filé powder after putting gumbo into individual serving bowls. Adding filé into the pot will make the gumbo too thick as filé powder acts as a thickening agent.

Marlow's CRAB SOUP

This is a great recipe that my sister Cori and her daughter Marlow whip up and is absolutely delicious!

Ingredients

1 pint whole milk
1 quart Half and Half
2 pints heavy cream
2½ pounds lump crabmeat
1 tablespoon fresh parsley
3½ teaspoons Old Bay seasoning
¼ cup unsalted butter
½ teaspoon salt
Cornstarch/water, add for your desired thickness

Directions

Bring milk, Half and Half, and heavy cream to a boil. Add crab, parsley, Old Bay, butter, salt and pepper. Bring back to a boil. Add the paste made from cornstarch and water to thicken. Garnish with fresh parsley and blue crab claws. Serve with a nice green salad or a grilled cheese sandwich on the side. Top with shots of hot sauce or sherry.

Playtime Coolers

My niece Marlow has her own special drink that she makes for her playdates. Enjoy!

Ingredients & Directions

½ a glass of pineapple juice
Add sprite to ¾ of the glass
Trickle in the cranberry juice
Add pineapple or orange slices into the beverage or on the side to garnish.

Part III
Inspiring Hospitality Message

I have been blessed over the years to be in the company of gracious women that have opened their homes, welcomed me into their community and provided me hosting advice along the way. They have inspired and taught me how to be gracious in welcoming people within my heart, home and community. Thank you to these wonderful women and I am excited to present their wonderful quotes that they have shared to inspire you.
Love, Dedra

Quotes from Family & Friends

As a young girl I remember how my mom, Kathleen Marlow, welcomed her guests, whether it was family or members of her community, with grace and generosity. She loved to have a beautiful home and enjoyed preparing for her guests. From polishing her silver, to setting a beautiful table, she made sure that all of the details were in place to make her guests feel special. She was a beautiful and gracious host, and for me, as a young girl, this was my foundation, and I am honored that the spiritual gift of hospitality has been passed on to my daughters. The spiritual gift of hospitality is a generational blessing. I am honored to be a part of this continuing legacy of faith, love, and humility toward others.
Blessings to you all, **Mary Daniel**

Hospitality can be shown at a large function, small private dinner party, or simply in the backyard. It is the people that make the event unforgettable. Show your guests warmth and a welcoming spirit and you will achieve true hospitality. One word comes to mind:
INCLUDE.
  Indulge in conversation. Share of yourself and open your soul.
  Never take no for an answer. Continue to invite those who at first say no.
  Community. A social unit of any size shares common values. It's ALL we have!
    Be part of your community!
  Listen and learn from your guests.
  Understand that everyone has a story to tell.
  Dive into your soul and share your innerbeing.
  Evolve as a hostess and you will evolve as a person.
INCLUDE *and welcome all different walks of life into your home. A smile, a simple nod, an invitation paves the way to a hospitable experience with you and your guests.*
With Love, **Bethann Mascatello**

I love opening my home—and my heart—to people I care about. For me, being a gracious hostess is about making the people in my life feel welcome, loved, and comfortable. It is with that spirit that I attempt to approach not only entertaining, but the gift which is given to us every time we awaken to a new day.
Love, **Elizabeth Reinhardt**

First, hospitality is biblical and commanded (Romans 12:13). That is, we are all called to honor God and demonstrate His relational nature. We show love because He first loved us (1 John 4:19). Second, we are to be the salt and light to a dark and dying world (Matthew 5:13–14). That is, the world is spiritually dead in need of the understanding of salvation through Christ and Christ alone (Romans 10:9). Opening our homes and tables to a weary world restores fellowship with mankind and allows us to share the good news of Christ. Finally, hosting others allows us to be missional and intentional about fulfilling the Great Commission (Matthew 28:18–21). While we may be busy moms that cannot go to the nations or elderly that want to testify but cannot travel, being a missionary right in our own backyard or at our own tables allows us believers to fulfill Christ's love and call in the world. Invite someone today for fellowship, food, and fun. Tell them about Christ and the work He has done in your life. You will be blessed. Hebrews 13:2: "Don't neglect to show hospitality, for by doing this some have welcomed angels as guests without knowing it." (HCSB)
God bless, **Toni Orrill**

Having the opportunity to make someone feel special. Taking their likes and dislikes into consideration when preparing for their arrival. They not only feel welcomed, they feel appreciated for who they are, as they are. Love, **Belinda Lee**

After years of praying for God to move in the hearts of people here in our rural community, it was a no-brainer to say yes to hosting Bible study at our home. All that we have is His anyhow. I continue to marvel at the immediate connectivity of those gathering to seek truth and fellowship. Even with our numbers reaching 60+ a week, there is intimacy throughout the home as our small groups meet in various rooms. Such a sweet sound to hear the discussions, the howling laughter, the murmuring of prayers. Can't think of a better way to bless a home and a community than saying, Bring it on!
Love, **Jennifer Andrews**

My son and daughter have always helped me in preparation when I am hosting in my home. It's become a family tradition and provides loads of fun for us. More importantly, it's a wonderful family adventure for all of us because we are acting with purpose to serve our guests out of love. This most recently manifested itself with something as simple as a "play date." I am filled with incredible joy each and every time my nine-year-old daughter Marlow thinks enough of her guests to automatically prepare a beautiful snack tray for them. Fresh fruits, crackers, cheese, and a delightful beverage that she loves to make—from pineapple and cranberry juice with a splash of Sprite—in her special glasses. Always a proud moment for me because she sees her friends and guests as very special too.
Love, **Corlessia Daniel**

As a young girl, I remember attending the Women's Society Meeting with my grandmother Daniel. This was an organization of Christian women who shared similar interests and genuinely loved each other. I was nine years old, so I did not know what to expect, but to this day, it is a memory I remember vividly.

When we arrived the door opened wide, and our hostess embraced us with a big smile then gave us a hug and kiss. I felt at home immediately. She took us into the family room; she thanked us for coming and began the meeting with a scripture, then the conversation led to warm conversation on various topics mixed with song and laughter. You could feel the love. After a period of time our hostess invited us into the dining room for lunch and continued fellowship. When you walked into the dining room, there was an aroma of food prepared from recipes that had spanned decades from family and friends who loved to cook as we shared in conversation while we dined.

The table was nicely set with pretty china and silverware—no plastic at this affair, with fresh flowers from her garden. There were other ladies in the kitchen that helped serve the food, replenish our punch and remove our dishes when appropriate so everything stayed impeccable and we all felt special with so much attention to every detail.

Always entertain with Love, in every aspect (planning, organizing, and implementing). It is a fool proof formula for creating a memorable experience that your guests will treasure for a lifetime, just because of the way you make them feel.
With love, **Angela Daniel**

Everyone needs a safe place to rest, rejuvenate, and feel refreshed. We consider our home a retreat where our guests can be spiritually and physically renewed. A few ways we prepare for their arrival is by asking them ahead of time for a list of all of their favorites, including breakfast items, drink selections, and special dinner recipes. We try our very best to accommodate most or all of these. It builds anticipation and excitement for them and us! We also prepare a gift basket for each room with a collection of books, oils, bath items, favorite snacks, and anything else we feel led to include. And lastly, we pray through the room as we prepare it with fresh linens and towels, asking the Lord to make their sleep peaceful and sweet and their stay with us full of love, joy, and whatever healing is needed.

Love, **Gloria Harding**

When I lived in Princeton, New Jersey, my children and their families would come to visit me the weekend before Christmas, and we would celebrate the upcoming holiday, leaving them free to do what they will on Christmas Day. We always had such a good time. When I moved back to the Washington, D.C., metropolitan area, I was excited to be back home among family. I wanted to nurture relationships, get to know nieces and nephews and their families and bring us all together. This motivated me to expand the Saturday–before–Christmas tradition my children and I had established, by inviting extended family and special friends to join us for a festive Annual Christmas Celebration (buffet style), known as Aunt Audrey's Christmas Party. The fellowship and singing of Christmas carols at this event helps to create my Spiritual Hospitality of a beautiful, peaceful, and loving atmosphere where guests feel welcome and special.

Blessings, **Audrey Smith**

Hospitality should start with our family. We often serve guests better than in our daily lives with our own family. I try to take each special occasion and embrace it at home. For example, the month of February when my children were little they made what we called a "love box." We took a shoebox and decorated it and then for the first two weeks of the month until Valentine's Day we would write each other love notes or thank you notes for the gifts we saw in each other. On Valentine's Day we would sit around the dinner table and open each one up. This box is still brought out every year and has traveled with us to other locations even for the weekend. It is important to share the love right in the home first. "The greatest gift that we give others is the love within," and that starts in our homes.
Much love, **Tina Boyd.**

My dad, James Wilson, was a true inspiration in how he lived his life by making others feel special in his company and making our home a loving environment. It is that spirit that I honor today in my daily life where I want people to walk into my home feeling special by seeing it and touching it. I like to add specialty items such as fresh flowers, pralines, and a good read in my guest bedroom. Hospitality is a gift that keeps on giving.
With love, **Angele Wilson-Gant**

SECTION III

COMMUNITY

☙

WE ARE ALL CONNECTED

Chapter 9
Light Your Candle

Share with God's people who are in need. Practice hospitality (Romans 12:13).

It's better to light a candle than curse the darkness (Chinese Proverb).

Are you aware of your surroundings? Are you lifting people through their suffering? Sometimes we read the newspaper or watch the news and we are disheartened by it. We discuss it at our dinner table and social gatherings, yet, we do not do anything about it. Do we take our own personal stance to lift those that are in need in our community? It doesn't matter what your socioeconomic situation is. There is someone that you can lift up, even if it is just to encourage them. You can bring light to darkness. With all of the turmoil that we have endured lately—tornadoes, hurricanes, military families that need support—our communities need a breath of hospitable grace.

When I stepped out and started praying for God to use me, His grace showed up in my work. He began to use me as a beacon of His hospitable grace. Right after Hurricane Katrina, a client and dear friend of mine called me and said that he wanted to do a Christmas tree lighting ceremony in his neighborhood to bring the community together. This was back in 2006, barely a year after the hurricane ravished the city. This particular neighborhood where my friend grew up and his parents lived, Pontchartrain Park, was totally devastated by the hurricane with 100 percent of the properties underwater. I was blessed to work with him because it was my first lesson in stepping out and letting God use me to create an event to be a symbol of hope within a community via hospitality.

I will never forget that night in the middle of Pontchartrain Park. We erected a 26 foot tree and a beautiful white tent that was draped in red where we had local choirs come and sing Christmas carols. The community brought special treats, such as hot cocoa and cookies. Excitement filled the air. As we gathered around the tree for the Christmas tree lighting, in the middle of a park surrounded by homes that were still marked with rescue signs from the hurricane, the community held hands, sang Christmas carols, and as they counted down three, two, one, the bright light of the tree came on. In that very moment, the light of Christ beamed so brightly, and you could see it in everyone's faces as they stood around the tree. The love of Christ was among them, and they had hope in their hearts for the future.

Today, the community is thriving. That night was a spark, and they have made leaps and bounds since. They are blessed to have leaders within their community that care, that love, and support one another, and that is evident in the people that come out of that community. They are making a difference in the world. Love the Lord your God with all your heart and with all your soul and with all your mind and with all your strength. The second is this: "Love your neighbor as yourself." *There is no commandment greater than these (Mark 12:30–31).*

Prayer

Heavenly Father,

As I step out of the comforts of my own home into my community, I pray to love my neighbor. Please ordain my footsteps so that people will see you through me. Amen.

Practice

Go and introduce yourself to a neighbor, find a homeless shelter, a school, a foundation that speaks to your heart, and volunteer where you can use your gifts and talents.

Pen

When you look at your community, what areas do you see yourself making a difference?

Research areas where you can volunteer and include your children if possible. The examples that we set now will influence our next generation.

Chapter 10
Heavenly Father ⊗ Use Me

For I was hungry and you gave me something to eat, I was thirsty and you gave me something to drink, I was a stranger and you invited me in (Matthew 25:35).

If God knocked on your door and said, "Join my team to share my grace through good works," would you take that leap of faith? Well, I'm here to tell you that there is a way to do good works. Letting the Holy Spirit guide you and use you will be astonishing in your life. Pray to God, ask Him to use you, and He *will* transform your life.

I had the experience of meeting a beautiful sister in Christ, Tina Boyd. Bethann, a friend of mine, said that she had a friend that I needed to meet because she knew that we would totally connect. I believe God gave Bethann that message to put us together, because when we finally met, we bonded quickly. Tina is one of those individuals that when given the "call to action," she will make things happen. Tina and I came together and there was an instant connection because of our love of the Lord, our families, and planning events. We both had been through some difficult times and were ready for healing and moving forward in our lives. When we are together, we are giddy with excitement as we come together to do God's work here on earth. It's not every day that people acknowledge what they have been gifted with by God and are able to come together to serve and be obedient and have a lot of fun, so we do consider our union a blessing.

Tina and I would often get together for tea in the morning after dropping off our kids at school, and we would use that time to pray. We discussed our aspirations and our faith walk and our yearning to serve. During one of our praying sessions, Tina showed up with an extra smile on her face and said that she had a bright idea. When she started sharing her vision to create an organization where we would come together and give back to the community and use our gifts and talents as event planners to make it happen, I was instantly on board. Thus, Women Walking In God's Spirit (W+winGs) was born. As we moved forward, Tina was moved by an article that she read regarding a young baby who almost died due to the mom mixing too much water in the baby formula because of her lack of financial resources. After researching the article and getting more information regarding food banks and how they often lack baby food, we quickly leaped into action.

Our initial goal was to create events to be a double blessing for the attendees. The first blessing was the opportunity of giving. We asked each attendee to bring baby food and formula which we donated to local food banks. The second was we always had speakers that focused on enhancing our lives spiritually, physically, and mentally. Tina and I put our hearts and souls into our events. Over time, Beth Kirk became a part of W+winGs. We hosted larger events where we had fashion shows for CASA Prince William County, Helping Haitian Angels, and a host of others. Each Thanksgiving and Christmas, Beth led our efforts by finding families in our community and we would have a breakfast for Thanksgiving where we asked all attendees to bring the ingredients, recipes, and cookware for each family so they could prepare their meals at home. For Christmas at our annual tea, Beth gathered the wish list from families, and our guests brought gifts that were wrapped at the tea and delivered afterward.

One year, my mom, daughter, and Beth dropped food off at a home where the grandmother was the caretaker. We prayed with them and in that moment, my mom spoke with the grandmother to give her encouragement and hope to let her know that she is not alone. This is what love for your community is all about.

This year, we decided to invite additional ladies into our fold in order to diversify our team and talents and we have created a board with wonderful women that are walking in God's Spirit. We are now an official foundation, and God is continuing to use us in many ways. This whole process has been a blessing from God. You see, we are women just like you, with hearts that love and worship God. We leaped on this journey because God called us to serve, and it is the most joyous feeling to uplift God's kingdom here on this earth. If He did it for us, He will do it for you. Just ask to be used.

Prayer

Heavenly Father,

Thank you for giving me gifts and talents where I can serve. I pray for discernment over my life to fully understand the gifts and talents you have bestowed upon me, so I can use it for your will and purpose. Amen

Practice

Take time to meditate and be quiet within your spirit to grasp the true nature of the gifts and talents that God has bestowed upon you.

Pen

What are your special gifts and talents that you can use to serve your community?

How do you feel that these talents can be used as good works within your home and community?

Do you have any friends and family that you can join with your gifts and talents to make a difference in your community?

Chapter 11
My Prayer for You

"Again, I tell you that if two of you on earth agree about anything they ask for, it will be done for them by my Father in heaven. For where two or three come together in my name, there am I with them" (Matthew 18:19–20).

Prayer

(Please fill your name in the blank area)

Dear Heavenly Father,

_____ and I humbly come to you asking for her/his heart to be open to receive God's love, and, in turn, that love will flow into her/his family, friends, community, and world. I pray that this is _____ season to breathe the grace of hospitality. I pray that her/his hospitable heart will be an example to others so they can join and be stewards to share this beautiful form of discipleship. Each day, I pray for light, faith, hope, peace, grace, mercy, vision, good health, provision, clarity, discernment, protection . . . and most of all . . . love over _____ life.

In Jesus' name we pray, amen.

Many blessings to you and your hospitable endeavors. May God continue to bless you and use you in mighty ways.

Your sister in Christ,

Dedra Faine

Acknowledgment

I thank God for putting the Spiritual Gift of Hospitality on my heart and using me to help share this beautiful form of discipleship. My husband, Roger Faine, has given me much encouragement, support, and unconditional love. My two beautiful children, Govan and Lauren, thank you for your love and motivation that inspire me each and every day. My father, James Daniel, although you are in heaven your loving spirit and presence is with me daily and I thank you. My beautiful mom, Mary Daniel, thank you for being my rock and keeping my home centered with your nurturing spirit. My siblings, Angela, Corlessia, JD, and Forrest, thank you for your love and support and a constant reminder that the Daniel Five are called to do great things. My beloved brother, Gregory, thank you for your constant love and support. To my business partner and dear friend Angele, you are a rock star, and I thank you for always being there for me and walking with me, I look forward to continuing to grow together with you. My wonderful girlfriends, Kimberly Jo, Lisa, Marcie, Tina and Toni thank you for praying with me, cheering me on, having a listening ear, encouraging me along the way, inspiring me, and most of all, for your love. Love you all!

To the beautiful women in my life that have inspired me by their example of grace and loving hospitable spirits–Hannah Daniel, Ruth Faine, Kathleen Marlow, Betty Welsh, Mary Basil, Debra Jordan, Frances Wallace and Linda Higgison–my heatfelt thanks.

Along the way, God has blessed me with wonderful people in the event industry that have supported my efforts. Steve Ornstein, thank you for sharing your beautiful flowers to help me tell my story. From day one you have supported me and I humbly thank you. Rodney Bailey, your gift of photography is a blessing, and I thank you for sharing your photographs throughout the book. Margaret Smith, thank you for listening to my vision and patiently helping me to bring it to fruition with your beautiful tableware. Karen Baker, thank you for your love, professionalism, delicious food, and constant support. To my wonderful graphic artist Sara Yokie, you are a delight to work with and your work is wonderful. Thank you for bringing my vision to life. It has been a blessing working with you all.

As I have walked through this journey, God has put friends and family in my life that have provided direction and wonderful support. Barry Beckham and Henry Stewart, thank you both for using your gifts, talents, and rolodex to help me along the way. Lance and Tina Boyd, thank you for opening your beautiful home for the photo shoots! Love you all!

Last but not least, thank you to my students who inspire me and bring me constant joy!

With love and gratitude,

Dedra

The following person(s) or business have been instrumental in producing this book. I am thankful and blessed to have each and every one of them working on this project with me:

Rodney Bailey
Rodney Bailey Photography
www.rodneybailey.com
703.440.4086

Steve Ornstein
Edge Floral Event Design
www.edgeflowers.com
301.340.0031

Margaret Smith
Capital Party Rentals
www.dulles.classicpartyrentals.com
703.544.8052

A La Carte Catering + Event Design
www.alacartecaters.com
703.754.2714

Sara M. Yokie
www.smydesigner.com

Thank you to the beautiful people that have appeared throughout the book. Tina Boyd, Marlow Buckner, Corlessia Daniel, Forrest Daniel, Mary Daniel, Govan Faine, Lauren Faine, Roger Faine, Queenie Johnson, Kaylan Kennon, Beth Kirk, Danielle Mason, Megan Mayer, Kendall Mayer, Lisa Miller, Kimberly Pugh, Victoria White

Celebrations from the *Soul*

For inquiries and to download our app *Gracing Up* please contact:

www.CelebrationsfromtheSoul.com

703.776.9003 (Phone)

703.776.9002 (Fax)

Dedra Faine is also the author of:

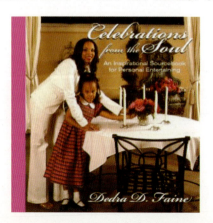

Personal Prayers

Personal Prayers